Things My Grandmother Taught Me

A Memoir for Soft Girls

Tamatha A. Davis

Things My Grandmother Taught Me

A Memoir for Soft Girls

Tamatha A. Davis

~Tamatha A. Davis

iii

Forward

~Tamatha A. Davis~

~ My mother, Ladell Tennon Hogan, was the crown jewel of our family.~

My grandfather, Porter Tennon, nicknamed my mother "Doll Baby". The reason - she was the most beautiful lady in all of God's creation. She had shimmering eyes, a contagious smile, and long curly black hair that was the envy of every lady in Texas.

My mother was more than the first lady of Hallettsville, Texas. As a nurse she won the hearts of not only her patients, but the citizens of Hallettsville. She used her network of friends and close associates to establish her church, Richardson Chapel United Methodist Church, as a historical marker in the state of Texas.

My mother was also a Tones. There were thirteen brothers and sisters who were descendants of Frank and Kitty Tones..

~Allan Hogan

~Tamatha A. Davi

v

~Things My Grandmother Taught Me~

Dedication
~ Dedicated to Ladell Tennon Hogan ~

This book is dedicated to the memory of the most elegant, beautiful, intelligent, kind, and loving woman I have ever known. She was everything that I still strive to be and more. I will never forget the beautiful divine lessons that she taught me. I am honored to be her granddaughter.

My grandmother when she graduated from high school at age 18 (year - 1948).

~Tamatha A. Dav[is]

Preface
~ My Grandmother was a Soft Girl ~

Through drafting this book, I realized that my grandmother was a soft girl. She taught me to be the same not through instruction but simply through living her life before me.

Here are a few things that let me know my grandma was a soft girl. She was all about self-care and treating herself. Some of the ways she treated herself were traveling, dressing in beautiful clothes and shoes, having her hair perfectly coiffed, and nails perfectly manicured every time she went out. She made herself a priority despite being the best mother and grandmother. Demonstrating for me what it looked like to really love and value yourself was a huge part of who she was. She lived life to the fullest on her own terms and taught me that as well.

I do want to be clear here because for my grandmother being a soft girl did not involve a man taking care of her. She did that for herself and quite well I might add. It was about the way she presented herself to the world. It was about her soft beautiful calm classy demeanor and speech that propelled her into rooms her socioeconomic standing would not have allowed her to enter. Remember, she was born in 1930 in the Jim Crow South.

~Tamatha A. Davi

Despite what you may believe, being a soft girl did not include being taken care of or neglecting financial responsibilities. Yes, she treated herself like a queen, but she did so on her own dime. I believe the soft girl era to be a beautiful one, but it should not neglect financial obligations. Like my grandmother, you can have it all, but you had better be willing to pay for it all as well. She carefully planned a life that allowed her to do that in abundance. I heard someone once say you can have it all just not at the same time. Those of you entering or already engrossed in your soft girl era, please consider this.

Yes, my grandmother was a soft girl- a soft girl with her own BE attitudes that I share in this book. What are your soft girl BE attitudes?

Contents

Things My Grandmother Taught Others

My Grandmother's "BE" Attitudes

Introduction
~ My Grandmother had her Own Beatitudes ~

Blessed are the poor in spirit: for theirs is the kingdom of heaven.

Blessed are they that mourn: for they shall be comforted.

Blessed are the meek: for they shall inherit the earth.

Blessed are they which do hunger and thirst after righteousness: for they shall be filled.

Blessed are the merciful, for they shall receive mercy.

Blessed are the pure in heart, for they shall see God.

Blessed are the peacemakers, for they shall be called sons of God.

Blessed are those who have been persecuted for the sake of righteousness, for theirs is the kingdom of heaven.

~Matthew 5:3-10~

These are Jesus' beatitudes that He shares in His Sermon on the Mount. However, my grandmother taught me how to live life well according to her very own "BE" attitudes. Most of the lessons I learned from her were caught not taught. This means that there were few times if any that she sat me down and said, "*I want to teach you about xyz."* Yet I learned more from her than anyone else in my life. Instead, I learned by watching her. Whether or not she knew I was watching her with the desire to learn from her and follow her, I will never know.

I will never know because she is with us in our hearts and minds always, but no longer here physically. She is with the One that she worshipped and served her entire life, the Lord Jesus. The bible says in 2 Corinthians 5:8 that when you are absent from the body, you are present with the Lord.

I am beyond thankful for every lesson that she passed down to me with her unique method of teaching - a method called living. I learned from watching the way she lived life, and my life became better because of it. And now, I shall share with you the seven lessons not only I learned from my grandmother, but lessons she taught others as well. These are the *Things My Grandmother Taught Me.*

~Things My Grandmother Taught Others ~

~Tamatha A. Davi

~ Granddaughters ~

I remember my grandma as one of the most peaceful, loving, and gentle spirits. She opened her home to all. She used to say to us, "Come on in here baby and meet your cousin." All rooms in her house were filled with laughter or freshly made food, especially peach cobbler.

When I got older, she showed me how to make that cobbler from scratch. It was her shining calm loving spirit that showed me how to follow in her footsteps and how to conduct life on a daily basis.
~Andrea Nowling, age 51

She was amazing and I loved her so much!
~Miracle Smith – Davis, age 8

~Tamatha A. Davi.

17

~ Nieces ~

Ladell Hogan, my paternal matriarch, was a person with the most beautiful soul! She provided a LOVE that was so pure and unconditional. It contributed to my understanding of TRUE love. I could not thank her enough even if I had all the words in the English dictionary. It would not be enough! She was more than an aunt. She helped lay the foundation for the person I am today – a strong, resilient, kind, nurturing, GOD- fearing, woman.

I will forever remember her teaching and honor her memory. I will display her shining light in my walk with GOD! I will love her into the heavens always!
~Candice Chapman, age 42

My special memories of Aunt Ladell were that she had listening ears, arms that hug and hold, a love that is never-ending, and a heart made of gold. She embraced me with a lot of love and support while growing up and even in my adult life.

After the passing of my mother, she was like a second mother to me, sprinkling love, warmth, and wisdom in my life. She was a gem and will be cherished throughout my life. She showed me what it means to live a life of fun, kindness, and generosity as well as the importance of cultivating a spiritual practice. That was a big part of her life that I subconsciously picked up on and carry with me to this day as I work to help others in the medical field.

As Big Mama would say "a little kindness can go a long, long way." This is how we learned to be a blessing to others.

**Proverbs 3:5: *"Trust in the Lord with all your heart, And do not lean on your own understanding."*
~Arethia McAfee Harrison, age 55**

**"Big Mama" was my grandmother's mother, Edna Tennon.*

Our family moved to the north end of Hallettsville, Texas in 1968, around the corner from our Porter Tennon family. Over the years of being in the presence of Aunt Ladell, I have been blessed to have an extraordinary aunt.*

The love, kindness, and wisdom that she shared was priceless. She was always so happy to see and visit with her nieces and nephews. She made us feel special. She probably did not know it, but she was a role model. It was always a treat to visit Aunt Ladell.
~Rosetter Tennon Burns, age 72

**Porter Tennon was my grandmother's father.*

Aunt Ladell appeared happiest when she was listening to her son and her daughters tell stories ... These cousins could all three spin the funniest stories ever. Especially her son would add a bit of high intelligence along with something funny that made us all laugh! She always had the cutest smile when they were doing this story telling. That is the time I enjoyed watching her the most.

Also, I am a walker. Often when I walk I think of Aunt Ladell. I tell people that do not know Aunt Ladell that I am channeling her energy through walking. As I age, I hope to continue to walk, thinking often of Aunt Ladell and channeling her energy for walking daily.
~ Bettie Hightower, age 73

~Tamatha A. Davi.

~ Friends ~

We were kindred spirits. When I think of her face I remember how the sweetness and love just radiated from her.

When I lost my only son, John, Ladell helped me to understand that God has a plan, and he does not make any mistakes. I do not know how I would have gotten through that time without her.
~Mary Ann Defibaugh, age 95

I met Ladell when we were in nursing school together. I was in my 20s and we were friends for over 40 years. We walked together in the mornings. We shopped together, and we traveled all over the country together. Despite our age difference, we were so compatible and just really enjoyed one another's company.

After I married and moved out of state, we still talked on the phone every Tuesday until her death. She was always interested in what I had to share. No matter how trivial it was, she would listen and tell me to just pray. Whatever the issue that was always her solution.

She was just one of a kind. She was an incredibly special person and so exceptionally beautiful inside and out. We were all blessed to have had her in our lives.
~Sandy Coe, age 63

My grandmother on a trip to Virginia with her friend Sandy Coe in the early 1990s.

My grandmother with her dear friend since first grade, Elolia Sampson.

~Tamatha A. Dav

25
~Things My Grandmother Taught Me~

~Tamatha A. Davis~

~ *Daughter* ~
Unconditional Love in Action

One of the many important qualities my grandmother instilled in me was to be loving. Not only did my grandmother teach me to be loving, but she taught my aunt, her daughter who was my mother's twin sister, Marilyn Rice, to be loving as well. My aunt Marilyn, whom we affectionately called Sugar because she was so sweet was the most loving woman that I ever met . She legitimately loved everyone that she encountered even those that mistreated her.

As the epitome of love in action, she lived her life freely and laid it down beautifully and gracefully for many around her. She never had any biological children, nor did she adopt any children, yet she was the most amazing mother that I have ever seen. As her twin sister's daughter, I was a recipient of that motherly love as were my children and many others.

She was a mother to the motherless. Any woman can love a child that she birthed, but it takes a special soul to love a motherless child. Her loving character was on full display in the lives of so many children. She even loved and cared for her former husband's nieces, nephews, and children from a previous marriage. He was a football coach, and she loved and mothered his players and students at the school as well. There were no bounds to the love she freely gave unconditionally expecting nothing in return.

My aunt demonstrated to me how to love everyone unconditionally. It was love in action. On Sunday mornings she would drive over to the projects in her town to pick up little girls that wanted to go to church. After church she would take them to eat and buy them treats and toys. One girl even lived with her for a while as a teenager when her mother was having difficulty with her.

She taught me love in action. Once she chartered a bus to take all the underprivileged children in the town to a theme park in the city. She bought school clothes for many of these children and often attended their school functions. She did all the things that a mother would do without the title and recognition for the most part.

She didn't mind because she was not doing it to be seen. She was doing it out of obedience and love for her Lord and Savior, Jesus Christ. She only concerned herself with what He thought of her actions because she knew that one day she would receive her reward in heaven.

A little over a decade ago she went on to receive that heavenly reward. I am beyond grateful that God allowed me to witness her beautiful, loving, genuine, generous, caring, gracious, soft life. She will forever be remembered and missed as my very beautiful and loving Sugar. She like my grandmother taught me to love

just like my grandmother taught her.

"The Twins" My aunt, Marilyn Rice (1952-2013) seated and my mother Marian Hogan standing.

~Tamatha A. Davi.

~ My Grandmother's "Be" Attitudes ~

~Tamatha A. Davis~

~ Be Kind ~

You have heard that it was said, 'Eye for eye, and tooth for tooth, But I tell you, do not resist an evil person. If anyone slaps you on the right cheek, turn to them the other cheek also. And if anyone wants to sue you and take your shirt, hand over your coat as well. If anyone forces you to go one mile, go with them two miles. Give to the one who asks you, and do not turn away from the one who wants to borrow from you. You have heard that it was said, 'Love your neighbor and hate your enemy.' But I tell you, love your enemies and pray for those who persecute you, that you may be children of your Father in heaven. He causes his sun to rise on the evil and the good and sends rain on the righteous and the unrighteous. If you love those who love you, what reward will you get? Are not even the tax collectors doing that? And if you greet only your own people, what are you doing more than others? Do not even pagans do that?
~ Matthew 5:38-47 ~

    If I had to pick one quality in my grandmother that stood out the most, it was her kindness. This was her mantra. Kindness was an essential part of her makeup. She had many other incredible qualities, but if her picture were in the dictionary it would be next to the word kind. This is the way in which she lived her life, and she taught us all to be kind and to live this way as well.

We were not people who got even, took revenge, or even made their point. We were too kind for that. She taught us that kindness ought to overshadow any other ways in which we desired to conduct ourselves.

I can remember my great-grandmother, my grandmother's mother often saying while sitting in darkness because in her later life she could not walk or see, *"Be kind. Do not be ugly or contrary."* I know without doubt that she is the one that taught my grandmother to live this way and they both inevitably passed it on to the next generation. There is a legacy of kindness in my family of which I am extremely proud.

The only fight (*if you would call it a fight*) that I ever had in my life was because of a boy. A girl was angry that her boyfriend liked me, or he was my boyfriend, and she liked him? I cannot remember. At any rate, there I was standing in the school hallway near the red lockers when she hauled off and hit me with a stack of folders right in the face I might add. I still remember how my face stung and how fresh hot tears began to water my eyes.

What did I do? I simply turned and walked away literally turning the other cheek. I became known for this incident – the girl that did not hit back when someone slapped her in the face. Although it sounds admirable now, I can assure you at that time it was far from it. It was something about which I was deeply embarrassed. You can blame my grandmother for this.

Throughout my entire childhood and adult life, I do not ever remember hearing my grandmother raise her voice. If she disagreed with something and she did often, she spoke in the same gentle soft voice to make her claim. She never responded in anger or even heightened emotions. I know she had emotions because I had seen her cry at church. But I never saw her express those emotions in anger – not once. She was too kind for that. My grandmother taught me kindness in action. She taught me not just the idea of kindness, but how to live a life of kindness in a world that is sometimes unkind.

~Tamatha A. Davi

~ Be Frugal ~

Do not store up for yourselves treasures on earth, where moth and rust destroy, and where thieves break in and steal. But store up for yourselves treasures in heaven, where neither moth nor rust destroys, and where thieves do not break in or steal.

~Matthew 6:19-20~

My grandmother was born in 1930. Many exciting new inventions entered society in 1930. Frozen food, Scotch tape and car radios only name a few! However, 1930 was best known for the Great Depression that began the year before on what history calls Black Tuesday. The Great Depression was a sad time in America's history. The stock market plummeted, businesses failed, and unemployment was rampant. People had difficulty just having enough to feed their families. Since my grandmother lived in a rural area where they grew and raised most of their food, she did not feel the effects of the Great Depression as much as those living in cities.

My great-grandfather worked in construction building highways for the government. His stable employment allowed him to provide well for his family at a time when almost everyone around them was struggling. My grandmother's family was often the first in the community to acquire modern technology like the telephone, indoor plumbing, and other conveniences new to society. Often people came to their home to use the phone and to watch television.

My grandmother's family were some of the few during that time that still did well. They never took any government assistance or handouts, and her father always drove a new car. He chauffeured his wife, my great-grandmother, around in it while she rode in the back seat.

Sadly, there were many people in her community in desperate need, and she saw their plight before her eyes. As a result of all she witnessed, not necessarily experienced, she became an extremely frugal person.

She never threw away any food. The food that we did not eat, she gave to the animals, usually neighborhood cats. Any food left after that went into her compost. According to Merriam Webster a compost is, *"a mixture that consists largely of decayed organic matter and is used for fertilizing and conditioning land."* Composting helped her garden to contain the best and most fertile soil to produce the choicest vegetables for her to eat.

Although she was quite comfortable financially, owning several pieces of land and earning a nice salary as a nurse having saved up for a comfortable retirement, she still only purchased items on sale. She was

compost. 2024. In *Merriam-Webster.com*. Retrieved May 22,2024, from https://www.merriam-webster.com/dictionary/compost

extremely prudent with her shopping and never wasteful. She said you never knew how the economy could change in a moment's notice, so you always needed to be prepared. She was a saver. *"Save your money for a rainy day,"* she said. All that saving paid off because in the end she was able to leave an inheritance for her children and grandchildren.

However, I know she was far prouder of the spiritual inheritance she left us than any amount of money. The spiritual inheritance she left was one of faith in God, reading and meditating on His Word, consistent prayer, faithful giving, obedience and belief in Jesus Christ, and serving and loving one's neighbor. Yes, those were the riches that were far more important to my grandmother.

Despite her being frugal, she was somehow still able to spoil herself. She traveled frequently on long vacations all around the country. She dressed impeccably and always maintained her hair and nails. And boy did she love shoes! How in the world does one spoil oneself while remaining frugal? And yet she did!

What a task! Yes, my grandmother taught me to be frugal.

My grandmother(Ladell), my mother(Marian), my daughter(Zoe) and me(Tamatha) on my grandmother's last ever major vacation – the "2016 Girls Road Trip". The road trip included 4 generations 10 days, and 10 states (Colorado, Wyoming, Montanna, Idaho, Oregon, Washington, California, Nevada, Arizona, & New Mexico).

~ Be Healthy ~

Or do you not know that your body is the temple of the Holy Spirit who is in you, whom you have from God, and you are not your own? For you were bought at a price; therefore, glorify God in your body and in your spirit, which are God's.

~1 Corinthians 6:19-20~

A serious incident occurred one day when my grandmother was on her way home from her daily walk. She walked three miles every morning. She told me that it was her medicine. The exercise, fresh air, and sunshine was the only medicine she ever needed up until her nineties.

However, on this unfortunate morning the neighbor's pit bull had gotten loose and as my grandmother was nearing home, he attacked her. She was able to grab a stick as she fell to the ground. Using that stick, she was able to fight him off the best she could until another neighbor saw her lying in the street and came to her rescue. She was able to get the pit bull away from them both and help my grandmother home. After that incident we all thought she would stop walking, but nothing would deter my grandmother from maintaining her healthy lifestyle. Less than a week later she was back out walking every morning again.

My grandmother also was careful about what she allowed into her body. I never saw her drink a soda or coffee and can count on one hand the times I saw her eat red meat. Keep in mind this a culmination of my entire lifetime, and I was nearing 50 when she passed away. Primarily, she ate the vegetables from her garden. Her daily food intake looked something like this:

- Breakfast: Cream of Wheat or oatmeal

- Lunch: Black-eyed peas or some type of beans and cornbread, sometimes a vegetable like okra, squash, or cabbage.

- Dinner: Add beans or a piece of lunchmeat (chicken or turkey) along with the vegetables and cornbread she had at lunch. Sometimes she prepared salmon croquettes or a piece of boiled or baked chicken; never fried.

Throughout the day she snacked on an array of fruit. Peaches, plums, grapes, apples, and cantaloupe were her favorites. She also enjoyed popcorn and various nuts. There were many pecan trees on our land, so, pecans were a staple for us all growing up and a healthy snack for her in the afternoons and evenings. She would also have hot or cold tea often in the evenings, and lots of water throughout the day that she drank out of her one special mason jar.

She rarely ate out. If she did, it was only when we, the grandchildren and children, would beg her to come along after some special function. On those occasions she always ordered the same thing – soup. Usually, it was the soup of the day. I believe she thought that the soup of the day was fresher. I am not sure if it was, but that is what she would order.

Her only downfall as far as eating if you had to pick one was sweets. She loved them! She loved all sorts, cakes, pies, cookies, and candies. She was an expert baker and enjoyed them quite often. She did not deprive herself of this one indulgence.

By example, each day my grandmother carefully taught me how to be healthy and the importance of taking care of oneself. She was serious about this, and she practiced what she preached every day of her life! This is the one lesson for which I wish I had paid more attention.

43

~ Be Forgiving ~

Then Peter came to Him and said, "Lord, how often shall my brother sin against me, and I forgive him? Up to seven times?"

Jesus said to him, "I do not say to you, up to seven times, but up to seventy times seven. Therefore, the kingdom of heaven is like a certain king who wanted to settle accounts with his servants. And when he had begun to settle accounts, one was brought to him who owed him ten thousand talents. But as he was not able to pay, his master commanded that he be sold, with his wife and children and all that he had, and that payment be made. The servant therefore fell before him, saying, 'Master, have patience with me, and I will pay you all. Then the master of that servant was moved with compassion, released him, and forgave him for the debt.

"But that servant went out and found one of his fellow servants who owed him a hundred denarii; and he laid hands on him and took him by the throat, saying, 'Pay me what you owe!' So, his fellow servant fell down at his feet and begged him, saying, 'Have patience with me, and I will pay you [all.' And he would not but went and threw him into prison till he

should pay the debt. So, when his fellow servants saw what had been done, they were very grieved, and came and told their master all that had been done. Then his master, after he had called him, said to him, 'You wicked servant! I forgave you all that debt because you begged me. Should you not also have had compassion on your fellow servant, just as I had pity on you?' And his master was angry and delivered him to the torturers until he should pay all that was due to him. "So, my heavenly Father also will do to you if each of you, from his heart, does not forgive his brother his trespasses."

~Matthew 18:21-35~

My grandmother had been a wife at one time in her life, and was a mother of three, so she obviously had relationships with men. Although I do not have details as she never divulged much about her past, I do not believe these men treated her with the love and respect that she so deserved. I do not believe the men in her life treated her in the honorable and loving way in which all women should be treated especially an extremely beautiful and intelligent woman like my grandmother.

I believe this is one of the reasons she learned in her life how to forgive and to forgive well. She practiced the kind of forgiveness the Bible speaks of where you do not keep the record of all the ways in which they have wronged you, and you pray for their success because you have moved far beyond the offense. No matter how unjust, abusive, disrespectful, or unloving it was, somehow my grandmother never held a grudge against anyone.

I know that she did not have an easy life. Raising a child without a father is not easy, and yet she raised three. She not only raised them, but succeeded in giving them an impeccable start in what was a challenging time in America's history for everyone especially a Black woman in the South.

My grandmother taught me the importance of education. I learned early on that the expectation was for me to be able to provide for myself when the time came. I was not encouraged to marry and have children. I think if anything, I was discouraged; education and career were paramount in her mind. The goal was not to marry well, but to do so well that you did not need to marry.

When I did decide to marry at a younger age, I can honestly say it was the first time that I knew without doubt that my grandmother was disappointed in me. I cannot blame her for that because we are all a sum of our experiences, and what we know of others' experiences. Unfortunately, my grandmother's experience with marriage or with men in general was not a good one. Consequently, her response was one that I fully expected.

When I became pregnant after three years of marriage, not only was she not happy for me; she was angry with me! I forgive her for that, but in that moment, she taught me another invaluable and important lesson - I had to live life on my own terms. We were different. In some ways our value systems were different, and that was okay.

I ended up losing that baby and even though she did not celebrate the life that my husband and I had prayed for and wanted desperately, I forgave her. At that time, I did not know that this would be only the first of three babies that I would lose, and I would never give birth or have biological children. I became a mom years later through the blessing of adoption.

Over the years my grandmother came to love my role as wife and mother. It is my belief that she experienced somewhat of a heart change. After adopting my children, she always encouraged me often saying that I was doing a wonderful job with them. How I valued and appreciated her words of approval and encouragement.

~ Be Loving ~

If I speak with the tongues of men and of angels, but do not have love, I have become a noisy gong or a clanging cymbal. If I have the gift of prophecy and know all mysteries and all knowledge; and if I have all faith, so as to remove mountains, but do not have love, I am nothing. And if I give all my possessions to feed the poor, and if I surrender my body [a]to be burned, but do not have love, it profits me nothing.

Love is patient, love is kind and is not jealous; love does not brag and is not arrogant, does not act unbecomingly; it does not seek its own, is not provoked, does not take into account a wrong suffered, does not rejoice in unrighteousness, but rejoices with the truth;]bears all things, believes all things, hopes all things, endures all things.

Love never fails; but if there are gifts of prophecy, they will be done away; if there are tongues, they will cease; if there is knowledge, it will be done away. For we know in part, and we prophesy in part; but when the perfect comes, the partial will be done away. When I was a child, I used to speak like a child, think like a child, reason like a child; when I became a man, I did away with childish things. For now we see in a mirror [c]dimly, but then face to face; now I know in part, but then I will know fully just as I also have

**been fully known. But now faith, hope, love, abide
these three; but the greatest of these is love.**

~ 1 Corinthians 13~

My grandmother loved. She loved hard. She loved well. She was known because of the love she freely shared with everyone. She did not reserve her love for her family only. On the contrary, she freely shared it with the entire community.

One example is Keith. Keith is my cousin's little brother. So, my cousin and Keith were siblings but had different fathers. I was related to my cousin through her father so technically Keith and I were of no relation. Therefore, he was not related to my grandmother either. However, if you told him that he would have never believed you! Of course, he was related to Aunt Lay as he affectionately called her. He was a young boy and my grandmother, now in her seventies, helped to care for him. In many ways she raised him as one of her own.

He came to her home every day after school and on weekends never left except to sleep, bathe, and eat. Early the next day he was right back there in his spot. And where was his spot? Her lap! She rocked many babies. It did not matter who their mother was, she was going to get them into her lap, rock them, and love on them as long as they wanted or in many cases needed. Keith was one of those babies. The only difference is he just never left. He never stopped wanting or needing her love.

As Keith grew, he became somewhat of a tall lanky fellow, and I know he had to be a teenager still crawling into my grandmother's lap, his legs hanging down in her rocking chair far past hers just allowing her to hold him. He would cradle his head against her chest into the nook of her neck as she rocked back and forth ever so gently. There was something special and calming in her embrace. I can still remember the look of peace and contentment on Keith's face. The look that says he is exactly where he is supposed to be, and to all of us watching, we knew that he was as well.

The love she had just oozed from her, and you could feel it. It was so strong that it was tangible. I experienced it as a child as well. Every child that was ever in a three-foot radius of my grandmother experienced it.

She did not have to grab them and pick them up as many older people had to do to get a hug. They just knew they were welcomed in her arms and would meander over to her and lean in until they were seated comfortably in her lap. That lap held so many over the years that I lost count.

She was everyone's grandma or Aunt Lay. She loved hard, and she was loved back just as hard. I believe children can sense when love is genuine, and that is what she had - a genuine love for everyone she encountered. She taught me how to love and to love well – to never stop loving no matter what. I must say that this is the lesson for which I am most thankful.

My grandmother at age 87 with one of the last babies she had in her lap – her only great-great grandchild – Miracle (year – 2017).

~

Be Humble ~

Do nothing from selfishness or empty conceit, but with humility of mind regard one another as more important than yourselves; do not merely look out for your own personal interests, but also for the interests of others. Have this attitude in yourselves which was also in Christ Jesus, who, although He existed in the form of God, did not regard equality with God a thing to be [f]grasped, but[g] emptied Himself, taking the form of a bond-servant, and being made in the likeness of men. Being found in appearance as a man, He humbled Himself by becoming obedient to the point of death, even death [h]on a cross. For this reason also, God highly exalted Him, and bestowed on Him the name which is above every name, so that at the name of Jesus EVERY KNEE WILL BOW, of those who are in heaven and on earth and under the earth, and that every tongue will confess that Jesus Christ is Lord, to the glory of God the Father.
~Philippians 2:3-11~

My grandmother was what many would consider a strong Black woman, and yet she was humble. She was strong because she worked extremely hard to raise her children alone. Yet in her demeanor, in her quiet and gentle voice, she was humble.

I learned that you do not have to be loud to be strong – to be respected in society. You do not have to yell and push your proverbial weight around. She taught me that there is strength in humility. There is strength in letting the other person win. There is strength in not getting your point made or even the final say. There is strength in prayer and in doing so allowing God to fight your battles. You see she did all those things and was still one of the strongest women I knew.

There is something to be said about mental strength. This mental strength helps you to stay silent even when you know you are right. It allows you to bow out gracefully from the fight because wisdom has told you that the fight is fixed, and you will never win – not in the way you want. It is better to just maintain your posture of quiet strength and dignity than to be brought down to a screaming match with another person. My grandmother never allowed anyone to bring her down. She taught me that sometimes the strongest thing you can do is exhibit humility by simply walking away. Humility allows you to walk away.

As a Black woman in the South, she was mistreated and looked down upon, and still held her head high. Remember the Civil Rights Act that gave her the right to vote was not passed until she was in her 30s. Even after that she still lived in the Jim Crow South. She was strong because she moved in spaces where she was sometimes unwanted, and yet she carried herself with a dignity and grace that is rarely seen. Yes, my grandmother was an incredibly strong, yet humble woman. She taught me about humility.

~Tamatha A. Davi

~ Be Your Best ~

Do you not know that those who run in a race all run, but only one receives the prize? Run in such a way that you may win. Everyone who competes in the game exercises self-control in all things. They then do it to receive a perishable wreath, but we an imperishable. Therefore, I run in such a way, as not without aim; I box in such a way, as not beating the air; but I discipline my body and make it my slave, so that, after I have preached to others, I myself will not be disqualified.

~1 Corinthians 9:24-27~

After my grandmother finished raising her three children and sending them off to college which was an impressive feat for a single Black woman in the seventies who only had a high school education, she determined to do something for herself. So, in her forties, she went to college. She knew that she could do more than clean homes, care for children, do hair, and take in laundry. Those are all noble pursuits if that is what you must do to provide for your family and that is what she did for many years.

My uncle recalls being angry with a boy at his school because he was able to spend more time with his mother than my uncle was. One of her jobs was working for a reputable family in our town: cooking, cleaning, and caring for their children. One of the children grew up to become the mayor of the town. My grandmother maintained a close relationship with that family until her death, and we all consider each other family until this day. Even though she lived her entire life in the South and her grandparents had been slaves, color still meant absolutely nothing to my grandmother!

At some point she decided that what she was doing to support herself was not her best. She decided that she could do more - be more. So she became a licensed vocational nurse (LVN). By the time I was born, this was her occupation, and this is what I knew her as – my grandmother, the nurse.

She worked hard at this endeavor and received awards for her abilities as a nurse as well as other pursuits within the community. Some of her achievements included:

- Nurse of the Year
  Texas League of Vocational Nurses

- Board member of Lavaca County Historical Commission
  Appointed by County Judge

- Founding member of Stevens Mayo Alumni Association

- Served her local church (Richardson Chapel United Methodist Church) in various capacities including usher and trustee for eight decades and was responsible for helping make it a historical landmark.

- Mother to three; grandmother to three, great-grandmother to six, great-great grandmother to one.

- Aunt and substitute grandmother to multitudes, and friend to all.

My grandmother taught me to always be my best. I never strived to make a specific letter grade in school. My goal was always to do my best, and that is what I did. As a result, I was always on the honor roll and received an academic scholarship to the University of Houston upon graduation, which I did not take. My mother felt like it was more important for me to get me out of Houston and on my own. We chose Southwest Texas now Texas State University in San Marcos where my uncle was an alumnus instead. I did continue to receive high marks in college.

Upon graduation, I was successful in my career field until I decided to stay home, raise and eventually homeschool my children. Through every pursuit the words that my grandmother passed down to my mother were always in my thoughts – *be your best*!

~ Conclusion ~

As I close this memoir to my grandmother, I believe I have done my absolute best for her. I pray that you will take the lessons I and others learned from her to heart – especially her "BE" attitudes:

- Be Kind
- Be Frugal
- Be Healthy
- Be Forgiving
- Be Loving
- Be Humble
- Be Your Best

My grandmother, Ladell Tennon Hogan, was an extraordinary woman; unlike anyone I have ever known. She taught me so much about life and how to live it well. It has been my absolute honor to share with you a portion of what she passed on to me simply by living her beautiful soft life before me.

I pray God's richest blessings for you as you pursue your best soft girl life as well. I was a witness to my grandmother's beautiful life, but in the end she lived her life before an audience of One – her Lord and Savior Jesus Christ. Live your life in such a way that at the end you have lived life to the fullest and enjoyed yourself.

However, most importantly you have lived to please Him - your audience of One.

"For by grace you have been saved through faith; and that not of yourselves, it is the gift of God; not as a result of works, so that no one may boast."
- Ephesians 2: 8-9

*"....for "*WHOEVER WILL CALL ON THE NAME OF THE LORD WILL BE SAVED.*"* **– Romans 10:13**

If you are unsure on where you stand in your relationship with God, please read the **Roman's Road** found in **Appendix A** of this book.

Appendix A
Romans Road

Keep in mind this is not a literal road or walk, but a spiritual one, which led my grandmother and me into the redemptive and powerful arms of the One that died for us all – Jesus Christ. This is the audience of One I mentioned. I'm inviting you to join us here:

Romans 3:23

"For all have sinned and fall short of the glory of God"

Romans 6:23

"For the wages of sin is death, but the gift of God is eternal life in Christ Jesus our Lord."

Romans 5:8

"But God demonstrates His own love toward us, in that while we were still sinners, Christ died for us."

Romans 10:9

"That if you confess with your mouth the Lord Jesus and believe in your heart that God has raised Him from the dead, you will be saved."

Romans 10:13

"For "whoever calls on the name of the LORD shall be saved."

Romans 5:1

"Therefore, having been justified by faith, we have[a] peace with God through our Lord Jesus Christ,"

Romans 8:1

"There is therefore now no condemnation to those who are in Christ Jesus, who do not walk according to the flesh, but according to the Spirit."

Romans 8:38-39

"For I am persuaded that neither death nor life, nor angels nor principalities nor powers, nor things present nor things to come, nor height nor depth, nor any other created thing, shall be able to separate us from the love of God which is in Christ Jesus our Lord."

Where are you?

Receiving Christ has nothing to do with your good works or moral behavior. It has nothing to do with your education, your family's pedigree, denomination or church affiliation. It has nothing to do with the church you attend or how long you have been a member, but everything to do with your relationship with God. ***"For there is one God and one Mediator between God and men, the Man Christ Jesus"* I Timothy 2:5**

Will you receive Jesus Christ right now?

Here is how you can receive Christ:

1. Admit your need (I am a sinner).
2. Be willing to turn from your sins (Repent).
3. Believe that Jesus Christ died for your sins on the Cross and rose from the grave. (Believe)
4. Through prayer, invite Jesus Christ, to come in and control your life through the Holy Spirit (Receive Christ as Lord and Savior).

How to Pray:

Dear Lord Jesus,

I know that I am a sinner and need your forgiveness. I want to turn from my sins. I believe that you died for my sins.   I invite you to come into my heart and life. I want to trust and follow you as Lord and Savior. In Jesus' name, Amen.

~Tamatha A. Davi

65

Appendix B
Grandmas' Peach Cobbler

Ingredients:

(for filling)
5-7 whole peaches
1 whole nutmeg
1 teaspoon cinnamon
1 cup sugar
1 stick butter
*Optional: the juice of 1
lemon*

(for crust)
3 cups all-purpose
flour
1 ½ cups shortening
¾ cup sugar
½ teaspoon salt
¼ cup ice water

Directions:
1. Prepare peaches by blanching
-Boil peaches whole for 1 minute
-Remove from heat and place in ice bath for blanching
-Blanching allows peaches to be peeled easily
2. Peel, core and slice peaches
3. Place in pot and cook over medium heat
4. Add butter, sugar and cinnamon
5. Grind whole nutmeg into the peaches using lemon
zester or small side of cheese grater
6. Use fork to break up slices of peaches while cooking
7. Pre-heat oven to 400 degrees
8. Prepare crust
-Add shortening using a fork to cut it in to flour mixture

-Slowly add ice water while kneading the dough
-Once all ingredients are combined to form dough separate in half
-Place one half on parchment paper and use rolling pin to roll out to size of your pan
-Place dough in the bottom of your pan
9. Now add peach filling to the pan
10. Roll out the other half of the dough on the parchment paper
11. Place the dough over the top of the pan with the peach filling
12. Bake at 400 degrees for 40-45 minutes until golden brown

Optional: Add melted butter, sugar and cinnamon to the top.

9 781733 057912